BEHIND
THE
SEALED
DOOR

Published in Cooperation with

THE METROPOLITAN MUSEUM OF ART

BEHIND THE SEALED DOOR

THE DISCOVERY OF THE TOMB AND TREASURES OF TUTANKHAMUN

IRENE AND LAURENCE SWINBURNE

SNIFFEN COURT BOOKS/NEW YORK

Color Photography by F.L. Kenett, reproduced by
permission of Robert Harding Associates, Bayswater,
London. Cover and black and white photographs on pages
9, 12, 25, 43, 70 (right), and 85 used by permission of
Griffith Institute, Ashmolean Museum, Oxford. All other
black and white photographs by permission of The
Metropolitan Museum of Art.

Cover design by Harry Rich
Text design by Ray Boultinghouse

Distributed by Atheneum Publishers, New York

ISBN: 0-930790-01-4
Library of Congress Catalog Card Number 77-88476

First printing October 1977

INTRODUCTION

Archeologists are explorers — people traveling on the sea of time to discover the past. They dig in the earth searching for objects used in long-gone civilizations. Even a piece of a vase can tell a great deal about life in ancient times.

Archeology is an important science. The more we know about the past, the more we know about ourselves. So many of our customs, so many of the things we say and believe, have their origins far, far back in history.

This is the story of one archeologist, Howard Carter, and his great adventure — an adventure that led him into a golden world that had not been entered for more than 3,200 years!

CONTENTS

THE MAN WHO STEPPED INTO YESTERDAY

Howard Carter first went to Egypt in 1890, when he was only seventeen years old. He went not as an archeologist but as an artist. His father was an artist and had taught young Howard to sketch. He had taught his son well, so well that he had been hired by the British Museum. And now the museum was sending him to Egypt to work with the famous archeologist Professor Percy Newberry. He would be sketching the items found by Professor Newberry in his explorations.

Like so many before him, Carter was fascinated by Egypt, especially the Egypt of long ago. He marveled at the huge pyramids, the ruins of the old temples, the mummies of the kings in the Egyptian Museum. He had the wonder and curiosity about the past that would eventually lead him to become an archeologist.

Carter worked for Professor Newberry, who in turn worked for Sir William Flinders Petrie. The world owes a great deal to this crusty scholar, for Petrie changed the whole science of archeology. Because of his precise methods, many more ancient objects were saved than would have been otherwise.

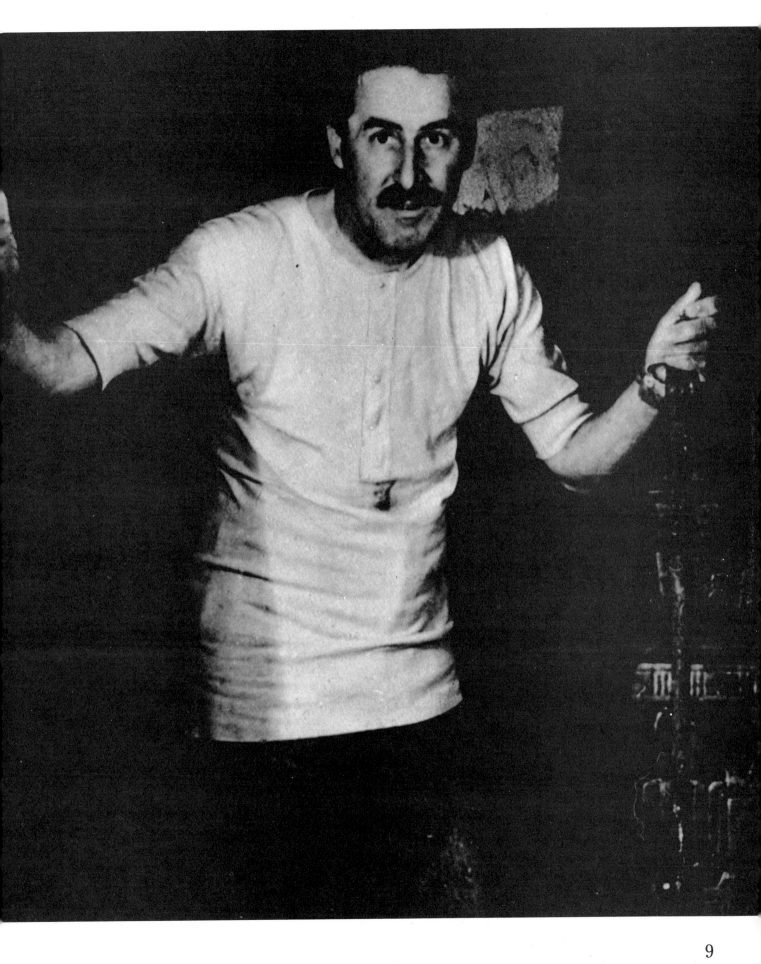

As a young artist, Howard Carter sketched this wall relief from an ancient Egyptian temple.

Before Petrie, archeologists had been very careless about Egyptian relics. They kept few or inaccurate records. They carried off precious ancient objects to foreign museums or private collectors. When they dug in the earth they often destroyed other treasures by sloppy shoveling. One even smashed open tomb doors with a battering ram.

Petrie changed all this. He insisted that the exploration be done with great care. Every bit of dirt had to be looked over; perhaps there was an ancient ring or piece of cup in it. It was said of Petrie that he sifted every spoonful of sand in Egypt. That isn't true, of course, but little escaped his eagle eye.

After years of working for Newberry and Petrie, Carter was offered a job with Theodore Davis, who was excavating in the Valley of the Kings. The site had this name because so many pharaohs (as the ancient Egyptian kings were called) had been buried in rock-cut tombs there. Carter jumped at the chance. After all, there was little more to be learned from the pyramids, those huge buildings that were the tombs of earlier kings. They had been robbed centuries before. But Carter believed there was still much to find in the Valley.

Working with Davis, Carter found, was very different from working with Petrie. Davis used the same careful methods, but he was not a professional archeologist. To him, archeology was merely a hobby.

Davis's digging crews worked in the Valley for twelve years. In that time he found several tombs. In one was discovered a sculptured head that is thought to be a portrait of Queen Nefertiti. It is considered by many to be one of the most beautiful pieces of art in the world. Yet Davis was disappointed not to find more. Many tombs were empty.

After a few years of archeology, Carter left it for a while. He returned once again to his art and spent three years as a painter.

Archeologists began searching for ancient treasures in this barren valley in the 1800's.

Then Carter met Lord Carnarvon. Like Davis, Carnarvon was very wealthy and interested in archeology. But his interest was more than a hobby. The English nobleman had been in a terrible car accident a few years before. His doctors ordered him to stay in Egypt for a good part of the year because its climate is warm and dry. And who could be in Egypt in those years without becoming interested in the many wonderful finds of the archeologists? For Carnarvon it became a consuming interest. It helped to keep him from thinking about the great pain he often suffered.

Carnarvon offered to finance Carter's exploration in the Valley, and so he returned to archeology.

It took a few months to get permission from the Egyptian Government, which would allow only one archeological group at a time to dig in the royal burial grounds. But once they had the permission, the two men and their Egyptian helpers started to work at once.

However, World War I broke out and digging went slowly. Tools that were made in England could not be gotten easily. Trained archeologists were not available. They were fighting in the trenches in France. But as soon as the war ended, Carter and Carnarvon went ahead at top speed.

Why Carter had set his heart on finding the tomb of the boy-king Tutankhamun is not known. However, years before, Theodore Davis had announced that he had found the tomb of Tutankhamun. Three clues led him to believe this. Near a small cave he had found a cup with Tutankhamun's name on it; then, a short walk away he came upon jars with the king's name on them; and in the cave was gold leaf, again with Tutankhamun's name on it.

Lord Carnarvon, Howard Carter's friend and patron, financed his Egyptian excavations for fifteen years.

Davis found objects left from the funeral of Tutankhamun in and around this pit.

But Carter did not believe this was Tutankhamun's grave. It was far too small for the last resting place of an Egyptian pharaoh. Yet Carter was convinced that Davis had proved the boy-king's tomb was not far away. And so the digging went on ... and on ... and still on.

At last Carnarvon, who had been so patient, became discouraged. By the summer of 1922 he decided to end the search. He invited Carter to visit him in England and told him of his decision.

Carter was not surprised by the news and was ready with a plan. He pulled out a map of the Valley and showed Carnarvon one small part below the tomb of Ramesses VI which they had not explored. He asked that the search continue one more season in this area. If nothing was found, he would bear the cost himself.

Carnarvon was so touched by Carter's determination that he agreed to finance one more season of digging in the Valley.

14

In those days the season for digging in the Valley was November through April. After that the heat made it impossible to continue working. But Carter knew he would have an even shorter season this time. His work blocked the entrance to the tomb of Ramesses VI, a favorite tourist attraction. He knew he would have to leave when tourists began to arrive in December.

The man in the lower left corner of this picture stands beside the pit that Davis thought was the tomb of Tutankhamun. At the right is the tomb of Ramesses VI.

On November 1, 1922, Carter was ready to begin his final dig. On the first day, he and his men uncovered a group of workmen's huts. By the fourth day they had removed the first hut and the sand beneath it. When Carter arrived that morning, a step had been discovered in the rocky floor of the Valley. By the next day, twelve steps had been uncovered, showing the upper part of a doorway — almost certainly the door to a tomb.

Carter needed all his self-control to keep from breaking down the doorway to end the suspense at once. After years of patient searching was this to be the discovery of Tutankhamun at last, or just another door with emptiness behind it?

This sunken step was uncovered the first week of Carter's final attempt to discover the tomb of Tutankhamun.

ROBBERS OF THE DEAD

Carter had good reason to be concerned about what he would find behind the door. Many times before, he and other archeologists had found tombs that promised great treasures. But when they were entered, the tombs had been empty. Someone, some group of men, had been there before them in the misty past and stripped the tombs bare. Who were these men? And why did they do it?

The great kings of Egypt built large tombs and piled them high with treasures. Jewels, precious oils, gold chairs and thrones, bracelets, rings, statues, the best of wines — all this and much more were stored in these final resting places.

Why did the kings hoard so much wealth in their tombs? It was because of their religion. Someday, they firmly believed, the gods would raise them from the dead. Also, they believed that they themselves were gods and would be welcomed into the land of the dead by their fellow gods. When that happened, they would need the things they had used in this world.

But, in fact, the kings would be very poor indeed when they arrived in the other world. Through the centuries grave thieves upset the royal plans and made off with the valuables buried in the tombs.

The thieves had no respect for the dead kings. They did not care if the rulers got to the land of the gods or not. They only cared about looting the riches in the tombs.

To get to the treasures, they had to dig through rock, break down huge doors, puzzle out mazes of passages that were found in the pyramids, and avoid traps that had been made to catch them. Often they bribed the guards to look the other way. The robbers did all this knowing that if they were caught, they would be horribly tortured and then put to death.

Because of their greed, many priceless objects have been lost forever — golden statues melted down and sold, jewels removed from their settings, works of art destroyed.

Between the years 2600 and 1529 B.C. the kings built enormous pyramids for their tombs. When a king died, his body would be carried into the tomb as high priests wailed funeral chants. But the dead king would not rest in peace for long. In a few years or even months, thieves would find their way to the heart of the pyramid where the king lay and carry off anything they could get their hands on. Even though probably many of the robbers were caught, just the sight of those massive tombs would remind others of the riches that lay within them, and a new gang would try its luck.

Huge pyramids, such as this one at Cheops, were built over the tombs of Egyptian kings in an effort to protect their mummies and treasures. You can also see the Great Sphinx, which has the head of a man and the body of a lion. This huge statue represented the god Horus, who guarded tombs and temples.

Finally, Tuthmosis I, who ruled from 1505 to 1493 B.C., realized a new way must be found to keep the royal graves from being looted. He decided to break with that long tradition and be buried in the valley which would be known as the Valley of the Kings. From this time on, the kings would be buried in tombs cut out of the rocky soil of the Valley.

You might think that the Valley would be a beautiful area, with shady trees, sparkling brooks, and flowers of every color. But you would be wrong. The Valley of the Kings is one of the most deserted and uninviting places in the world. Its landscape consists of brown rocks and brown sand. It has no trees, no streams, and no flowers. Few birds fly into this forbidding cemetery. However, it was much easier to protect than the pyramids.

Hundreds lived or worked in the Valley. There were men who did the heavy work of digging into the rock. There were craftsmen who performed such jobs as painting the walls of the tombs. There were the priests who were in charge of all activity in the Valley. And, of course, there were the soldiers, whose duty it was to keep out the thieves. The most important work was that of the mummifiers, people who made the kings' bodies into mummies. Mummifying is a process which can preserve bodies for hundreds, sometimes even thousands, of years.

The ancient Egyptian skill of mummifying has fascinated people up to our time. After the body had been specially treated, it was dried, a process that took seventy days. Then it was washed with special sweet-smelling oils. The body was carefully wrapped in linen. The linen had been soaked in gum, a sticky substance that came from a gum tree. Metal charms and special prayers on papyrus were enfolded in the wrappings. There was plenty of room for these items, for the linen was wound around the body many times.

The exact location of a king's tomb was usually kept a secret — though, of course, some people had to know about it. Tuthmosis I assigned a trusted official, Ineni, to prepare his tomb. Ineni carried out his duty faithfully. As he wrote later, "I alone supervised the construction of His Majesty's cliff tomb. No one saw it, no one heard it."

But Ineni could not have possibly dug this huge cave by himself. What probably happened, according to Howard Carter, was that a hundred or more slaves did the work and then all of them were killed.

But nothing stopped the tomb robbers. In fact, the thieves became so successful that sometimes the priests, hoping to fool them, would have the royal

mummies moved from cave to cave. Several mummies might be stored in one tomb for a time while other tombs were empty. This created puzzles for archeologists much later, who might find the tomb of one king occupied by a different king's mummy.

The ancient Egyptian civilization lasted for over 3,000 years. Yet finally it too came to an end. At various times after that, other nations conquered the country, but the work of the tomb robbers continued as before. It was as if they had discovered an

Thirty or more kings were buried in this lonely, forbidding valley known as the Valley of the Kings.

Sixteen steps led to a sealed doorway. Behind it, Carter hoped to find the tomb of Tutankhamun.

unending goldmine in the Valley of the Kings, and through the centuries they searched for undiscovered graves of kings.

By the late 1800s the Valley had been gone over carefully, and many archeologists believed that nothing more would be found. However, in 1871 they were surprised to learn that objects of great value were being sold by people who lived on a hill near the Valley of the Kings. Experts agreed that these objects could only have come from the tombs of kings.

After some very clever detective work, it was found that most of the objects had been sold by a man named Abd-el-Rasul.

Abd-el-Rasul was arrested, and he confessed that he had been the seller of the valuable relics. Even more amazing was his statement that for years the entire income of the village of Qurna had been derived from selling such relics. What's more, his family had been in this business for six centuries!

Recently his people had found a tomb high on the face of a cliff. It could be entered only through a small hole, into which a thin man could squeeze. Hoping to please the officials and avoid a long jail sentence, he offered to lead the way to the grave.

Forty mummies were found in the small tomb! The mummies were taken to the Cairo Museum. As the boat carrying the remains of the kings passed down the Nile, hundreds of thousands of Egyptians lined the banks of the great river. They threw dust upon themselves, a sign of mourning. People fired rifles in the air in salute. All this was done to honor these dead kings who had ruled some 3,000 years before.

But that was not the end of the grave thieves. Even during the years that Howard Carter searched for new tombs in the Valley, the robbers were searching, too.

And so as Howard Carter descended the newly uncovered steps and stood before the sealed door, he had reason to wonder. Was it possible that this tomb had remained undiscovered for over 3,000 years?

This was Carter's first glimpse of the treasures that lay inside the tomb. The gate was added later to protect the contents.

WONDERFUL THINGS

Howard Carter did not enter the tomb right away. First he sent a telegram to Lord Carnarvon, asking his friend to come quickly. If it really turned out to be Tutankhamun's tomb, he did not want Carnarvon to miss the moment of opening it.

Today it would take only a few hours to travel by plane from London to Egypt. But few people flew in 1922. Carnarvon had to make the journey on trains and ships. For more than three weeks Carter waited. Finally the English nobleman and his daughter arrived.

At the site, all was ready. Carefully the outer door was removed. Before them was a passage, and then another door. Carter drilled a hole in this second door. He held a candle inside, and for the first time in more than 3,000 years light pierced the darkness. He saw all kinds of strange objects. Everywhere was the glint of gold.

Carter was unable to speak for a moment.

"Can you see anything?" asked Carnarvon.

Carter forced out the words. "Yes. Wonderful things!"

It was, Carter wrote later, "the day of days, the most wonderful that I have ever lived through."

At first sight the room looked something like an untidy attic or basement storeroom.

Treasures lined the walls of the Antechamber in the tomb of Tutankhamun. Never before in Egyptian archeology had so many precious objects been found. Carter's discovery was truly the greatest find, well worth the long years of searching.

27

Four golden chariots lay dismantled in a corner to the left of the entrance to the Antechamber. According to the ancient Egyptian religion, Tutankhamun could use these chariots in the land of the dead.

Apparently thieves had broken into the tomb, and in their search had scattered things about. Whoever had discovered the robbery — priests, guards — had put back the objects in a hurry. The door had then been sealed again. Perhaps it was at that time that the tomb was buried and workmen's huts built over it so as to fool any later thieves. This was a fine idea, and we owe a great deal to the person who thought of it. Otherwise, Carter would not have found the

Against the back wall stood three beautiful golden beds carved in the shape of animals. Magnificent chests and boxes filled with treasures were among the objects piled on and under the animal beds. Clay boxes containing food can be seen stacked under the center bed.

Carter quickly noticed the darker area of the wall between the two large statues. This was another sealed doorway which he hoped would lead to the mummy of Tutankhamun.

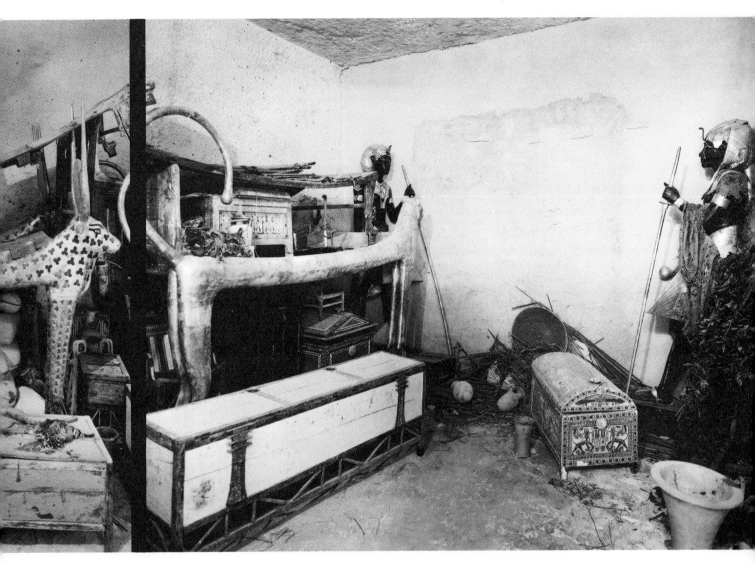

tomb's great treasures.

Carter guessed at once that another room containing the mummy of King Tutankhamun had to be connected to this first room. It did not take him long to find it. It was tempting to go through this third door, but Carter was a careful and dedicated scientist. He knew he had to clear the Antechamber, which was filled with valuable objects, before going into the rooms beyond.

Carnarvon and Carter realized that they and their Egyptian workers needed more professional help to catalog and safely pack their great find. Another group of archeologists was in the area. This group had been sent there by The Metropolitan Museum of Art in New York. Carter asked the museum officials if he could "borrow" Harry Burton, a photographer, for a while.

Some archeologists might have been jealous

Harry Burton made over 1800 photographs of the treasures found in the tomb of Tutankhamun. Most of the black and white photographs in this book were taken by him.

The chariots found in the Antechamber were among the objects repaired and restored in a nearby tomb by Arthur Mace, a member of the staff of The Metropolitan Museum of Art.

enough to refuse. But the officials of the Metropolitan Museum were quick to see the importance of Carter's work. They not only sent Burton, but three other people besides.

Before any object could be removed, photographs and sketches had to made showing the room and the treasures exactly as they were found. Once the room was cleared, the photographs and drawings would be the only records left to show their original location and condition. Carter knew, too, that sometimes ancient objects that appear to be in perfect condition can collapse into dust when touched, and in that case the photograph would be all that remained. A darkroom was set up in a nearby tomb so that Harry Burton could develop the photographs immediately to make sure they were satisfactory before the object was touched. Sometimes dozens of photographs had to be taken to get one that was satisfactory.

Once the treasures were photographed and sketched, the job of removing them could begin. Each one was loaded onto a padded wooden stretcher and fastened to it with linen bindings. Then the stretchers were carried under guard to a laboratory which had been set up in the empty tomb of Sety II in another part of the Valley. There they were cataloged, repaired, and restored before being shipped to the Cairo Museum.

This large animal bed had to be taken apart before it could be removed from the tomb, safely placed on a stretcher, and carried to the laboratory nearby.

Whenever possible, Carter kept the objects visible on their stretchers so that the tourists who had waited for hours in the sun could be rewarded with a glimpse of these priceless treasures as they emerged from the tomb.

It took seven weeks for the hundreds of objects in the Antechamber to be photographed, listed, carefully packed and removed to the laboratory.

Visitors watch as chariot wheels are removed under guard from the tomb.

On the following pages are some of the many beautiful and interesting objects Carter found in the corridor and the Antechamber.

The statue of a sun god on a lotus was found just outside the Antechamber. The Egyptians believed that once everything was a huge ocean called Nun. There was no land, no animals, no people. Then one day a mound appeared in the Ocean of Nun and on it grew a beautiful blue lotus. Out of the lotus grew a god, and this god became the sun.

33

This object, made in the form of a lotus, was thought to be Tutankhamun's drinking cup. It was carved from a single piece of alabaster. The handles are lilies. Part of the inscription in hieroglyphic writing reads, "May your spirit live and may you spend millions of years . . . sitting with your face to the north wind, your two eyes beholding happiness."

This wooden chest is brilliantly decorated with scenes of war and hunting. It contained over fifty objects, mostly clothing such as sandals and robes.

This trumpet may have been made to be used in battle. The exact sound heard in ancient times can be reproduced today on it. The stopper was covered with a cloth, thrust into the trumpet, and twisted around to clean it.

These large golden animal beds were the first objects Carter saw as his light shown into the Antechamber. Their heads cast eerie shadows on the walls. The beds were too tall to have been used as ordinary beds. It is possible that they were used during the mummifying process.

The heads of the three golden beds were carved in the shape of a hippopatomus (top left), a cow (top right), and a lioness (lower left).

The king's "dummy" of painted and stuccoed wood has a lifelike appearance. He is shown wearing the flat-topped crown of Lower Egypt. Lower Egypt was that part of the country near the Mediterranean Sea. Upper Egypt was the southern part of the country. Once these sections were separate nations, but they had been unified centuries before Tutankhamun.

At times, Egyptian priests wore leopard skins. This leopard's head was worn on such a robe. Since Tutankhamun was also a priest according to the ancient Egyptian religion, he was allowed to wear the leopard skin. One was found in the tomb, but it was in poor condition.

This folding headrest of ivory is decorated with heads of protective gods. The legs of the headrest end in ducks' heads. Headrests were very important to the Egyptians. They believed that the head was where life really existed.

Sticks decorated with figures representing African and Asian enemies of the king are thought to have been used in parades. The king would drag them behind him in the dust to symbolize his triumph over his enemies.

This small box was a shrine to the vulture goddess Nekhbet. On the sides of the box are scenes from the life of Tutankhamun. In one scene Tutankhamun stands on land and shoots arrows at birds rising from a swamp. The queen is handing him arrows.

Once the shrine contained a statue of Nekhbet. Two small holes for the goddess's feet are on the pedestal inside. Like the shrine, the statue probably was made of silver and gold. No doubt a thief took it away.

39

The gilt throne of Tutankhamun is decorated with a scene showing the young queen anointing the king with perfume. The rays of the sun god shine on the couple. Behind the queen stands a large bead collar.

Life-size statues of
Tutankhamun stood guard
at each side of the sealed
door to the Burial
Chamber. Black is the
color the Egyptians
associated with rebirth.
The statues may have
been painted black to
assure Tutankhamun life
after death.

BEHIND THE SEALED DOOR OF THE BURIAL CHAMBER

Opening a passage to the Burial Chamber was as exciting as entering the Antechamber, maybe even more exciting, because the coffin of Tutankhamun was inside. Or was it? Perhaps the thieves had stripped the Burial Chamber of all its treasures even though they had left a great deal in the Antechamber.

This time Carter and Carnarvon were not alone. The objects of the Antechamber had all been removed except for the sentinels. Now the room was filled with many Egyptian officials and famous archeologists, who watched as Carter slowly tapped on the blocked doorway with a hammer.

When he had a large enough hole, he flicked on a flashlight and peered within. What he saw almost took his breath away. Later he wrote that it seemed as though he were staring at a wall of gold.

Actually he was looking at a huge box or shrine that filled almost all the space in the Burial Chamber. The shrine had been coated with gold.

*The sentinals stand guard
beside the opened doorway
to the Burial Chamber.
The huge golden
shrine can be seen inside,
almost filling the Chamber.*

44

When Carter found this graceful lamp, traces of oil could still be seen inside it. The lamp was carved from a piece of alabaster in the shape of a lotus plant.

When the doorway was completely opened, Carter and Lord Carnarvon had the honor of entering first. Carter edged his way around the magnificent shrine, which gave him only a narrow passageway between it and the wall. Two beautiful vases lay blocking their path. Carefully Carter marked their location and passed them back into the other room.

Finally they found the shrine doors, and their hearts plunged with disappointment. The doors were not sealed! The thieves had penetrated this far.

Had they taken everything? Slowly the two men pulled the doors back . . . and saw another set of doors.

This huge shrine had been put together
in the Burial Chamber. Then a wall between
the Burial Chamber and the Antechamber
had been built. The shrine so nearly filled
the room that great skill and patience would
be needed to dismantle it without damage.

The original seal of the officials who guarded the Valley can be seen at the right-hand side of the cords. The seal shows a jackal over nine captives.

To their delight the doors of the second shrine were fastened with ropes and stamped with the unbroken seal of the official guards of the Valley. The robbers had reached no further. Carter and Carnarvon knew that within this shrine lay a world

untouched for nearly 3,300 years. Of the many
kings buried in the Valley, Tutankhamun alone
throughout the centuries remained undisturbed —
sheltered within those dazzling golden shrines.

The photograph below shows objects heaped on the floor between the first and second shrines. A linen curtain which had covered the second shrine can be seen in front of a large alabaster perfume vase. The lion jar, shown in color on the next page, is also visible in this photograph.

On the ground inside the doors of the first shrine was an alabaster jar with a lion on top. When Carter found it, it still held some cosmetics placed there when the king was buried. Carefully carved heads formed the four feet of the jar. Each head represented an enemy whom the Egyptians had conquered.

This beautiful double box held valuable ungents. The two seated figures represent Tutankhamun wearing the side braid of a prince.

Near the lion jar lay a double box of gold inlaid with glass paste. It shows the king seated holding the royal insignia of crook and flail.

Carefully Carter closed the great doors. He could go no farther until the next season when the outer shrine could be safely dismantled.

The two men silently continued along the passageway. Along one wall they came upon eleven paddles and oars. The Egyptians believed that the king would need them to row himself across the waters of the underworld.

Paddles and oars lay in the narrow passageway beside the shrines.

A small inner room off the Burial Chamber was filled with treasures. Its unsealed doorway was guarded by Anubis, the jackal god.

At the farther end of the Chamber the men saw another door. This one had not been blocked and sealed. A single glance was enough to assure them that this small room contained the greatest treasures of the tomb.

After Carter and Carnarvon had surveyed the small treasury, they returned to the Antechamber. In twos and threes the waiting guests were allowed to enter the Burial Chamber. No one spoke above a whisper. When they all came out of the tomb into the sunlight, they looked around as if in a daze. No one was able to find words to describe the wonders they had seen.

Shortly after that day, in the nearby city of Luxor, Lord Carnarvon was bitten by a mosquito which apparently carried a disease. Never in good health since his automobile accident twenty-five years before, he developed a fever and soon died.

Howard Carter deeply missed his partner and good friend, but he was determined to carry on.

The next season Carter began the difficult task of removing the huge outer shrine. It was seventeen feet long, eleven feet wide, and nine feet high. The shrine had been brought into the Chamber in sections and then put together. It would have to be removed in sections also. Scaffolding and hoisting tackle were set up inside the crowded Chamber to assist in the removal of these massive sections weighing as much as 1500 pounds.

When the outer shrine was removed, the linen curtain covering the second shrine was treated with chemicals to keep it from disintegrating. It was then rolled onto wooden rollers and removed to the laboratory.

With the outer shrine and the curtain removed, Carter was able to inspect the second shrine. It was very similar to the first shrine. Its sides had been decorated with beautiful scenes to guide Tutankhamun on his journey to the underworld and to explain the evil powers he would meet on his route to the land of the blessed.

Carter and his aides remove sections of a shrine. Working in a limited space without damaging the delicate panels was a long and difficult task.

The goddess Isis carved on the door of the third shrine spreads her wings to protect Tutankhamun's mummy. Magic spells are inscribed on the door. They promise the king everlasting life.

Carter at the open doors of the second shrine inspects the third shrine inside. It had been sealed in the same manner as the second shrine.

Carefully Carter cut the cords fastening the doors of the second shrine and removed the precious seal. When these doors were opened, Carter found a third shrine. The doors of the third shrine had been fastened and sealed just as the second had, and the seal was also unbroken. When the cord had been cut and the seal removed, the doors were opened to reveal a fourth and even more beautiful shrine inside.

Through the open doors of the shrines a stone sarcophagus can be seen.

Carter called this moment indescribable. What would this fourth shrine contain? With great excitement the bolts of the unsealed doors were drawn back and the doors swung slowly open.

Inside was a huge stone chest called a sarcophagus. At each of the four corners was carved a goddess with wings spread and arms circling the sarcophagus as if to keep away intruders.

Goddesses with wings outstretched stand at each corner of the sarcophagus to protect Tutankhamun.

It was a month before the remaining shrines could be removed from the Chamber and the sarcophagus could be opened. Carter and his aides stood in silence as the huge stone lid was slowly hoisted in the air. It was the moment they had all been waiting for since they had first discovered the tomb two years earlier. At last they were to see how a king was buried in ancient Egypt. What would they find inside this giant vault unopened for 3300 years?

Their first look into the lighted vault was disappointing. Linen wrappings completely covered whatever was inside. But when the linen was removed, the sight was far from disappointing. It was a magnificent golden coffin. Its shape was that of the god Osiris, but the face was Tutankhamun, the boy king.

The outer coffin of Tutankhamun lies wrapped in linen inside the sarcophagus.

The coffin was seven feet long and completely filled the sarcophagus. The body was a feathered golden surface but the face and hands were smooth. They had been beautifully sculptured and covered with sheets of gold. The hands held the royal crook and flail. On the forehead were the cobra and vulture, symbols of Upper and Lower Egypt, circled with a tiny wreath of flowers.

Carter wrote of that moment: "In the silence, you could almost hear the footsteps of the departing mourners."

Carter and his party lowered their lights and once again climbed the sixteen steps dividing the past and present.

Here the outer coffin is shown after the linen was removed.

*A small wreath of flowers
circles the vulture and cobra
on the outer golden coffin of
Tutankhamun.*

When work began the following season, the first task was to lift the lid of the coffin as it lay in the heavy sarcophagus.

As the lid was carefully hoisted, a second coffin

could be seen inside. It was fitted in so tightly that even a small finger could not be put between it and the first coffin. This second coffin was wrapped in linen and strewn with flowers.

The top and bottom of the outer coffin were held together with solid silver tongues fitted into the openings that can be seen here. Gold headed pins held them in place.

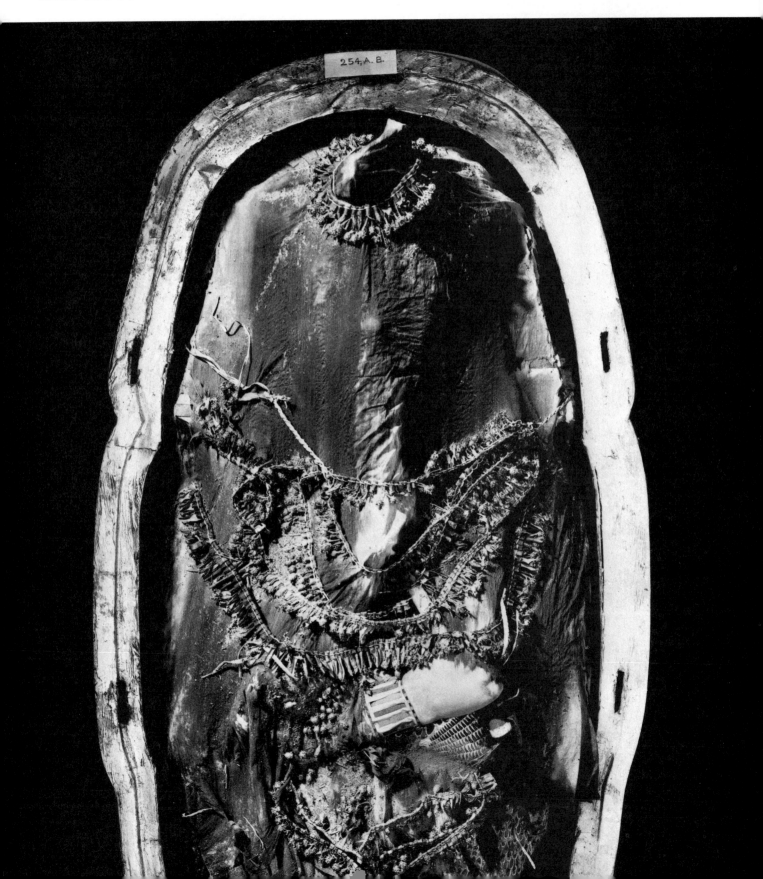

When the linen was taken off, they saw not the mummy of the king but another coffin, also shaped like Osiris and again with the face of Tutankhamun.

Carter examines the magnificent
workmanship of the second coffin.

    This coffin was even more beautiful than the first.
It was also wooden and covered with gold leaf. But
unlike the first coffin, this one was inlaid with colored
glass fitted into strips of gold.

Because it fitted so tightly into the first coffin, removing it was difficult. The second coffin could not be raised safely out of the first, so Carter lowered the first coffin. This left the second coffin free and gave Carter a full view of this magnificent work of art.

The color photo on the next page shows the second coffin after it was cleaned.

With great difficulty the lid of this coffin too was removed. And now Carter made the greatest discovery of the tomb. Inside there was yet one more coffin, the true resting place of the golden king. This six-foot coffin was made of solid gold and weighed 222 pounds!

Carter removes the linen covering the third coffin. Many precious objects were to be found in the linen wrappings.

The mystery of the heavy weight of the coffins is solved when Carter discovers that the third coffin is made of solid gold.

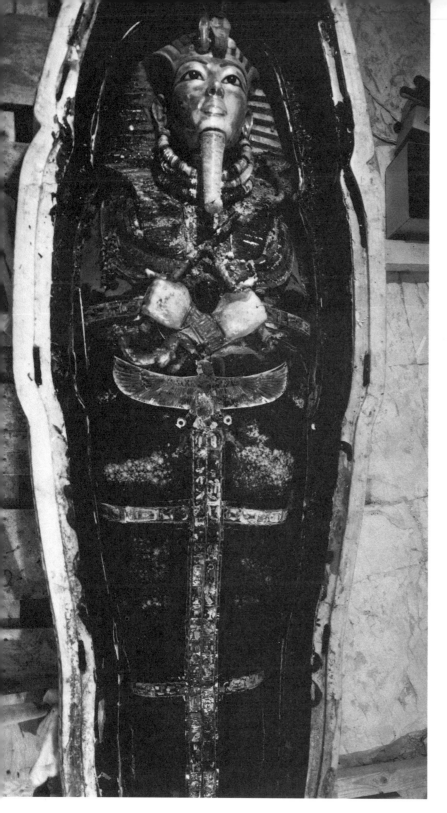

Howard Carter was awed by the sight of the beautiful mask. "Three thousand years and more had elapsed since men's eyes had gazed into that golden coffin," he wrote.

The mask fit over the head and shoulders of Tutankhamun's mummy. In this photograph the beard had not yet been replaced after cleaning the mask.

Inside was the mummy. Covering the head of the long-dead king was a magnificent mask, also made of solid gold.

Few kings in the history of the world, however rich beyond imagination, ever had anything like this mask. Experts agree that it is one of the greatest works of art ever found.

The rest of the mummy was wrapped in linen. Within the cloth were more than a hundred precious jewels and beautiful daggers made of gold.

These two daggers with gold sheaths were found in the linen wrappings of the mummy shown on the page at left. The blade of one is gold, the other iron.

The handle of the gold dagger is decorated with a carved pattern and glass and stone inlay.

73

Many important and precious funeral objects were found in this small room off the Burial Chamber.

THE FINAL ROOMS

After the coffins and shrines were removed, Carter and his helpers explored the small room off the Burial Chamber. Carter had named it the Treasury after he had first glimpsed the richness of its contents.

The statue of the god Anubis lay in front of the open door of the Treasury. From this spot he could watch over the mummy of Tutankhamun and protect the objects placed in the Treasury to assure Tutankhamun a safe journey through the underworld and into the life beyond.

Behind Anubis was the head of the sacred cow representing the goddess Hathor.

In the center of the wall facing the doorway was the most important object in the Treasury, the golden shrine. Carter described it as the most beautiful monument he had ever seen. It was completely covered with gold. Its top was decorated with a series of cobras inlaid with colored glass.

On each of the four sides of the shrine stood a goddess of the dead, gracefully guarding the contents. Inside the shrine was an alabaster chest containing four miniature coffins. These tiny coffins held the internal organs of the king which had been removed during the mummifying process.

On the pages that follow are some of the beautiful objects crowded into the small Treasury.

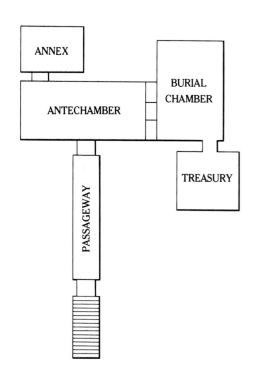

The wooden figure of a jackal represents the god Anubis. From his position in the doorway of the Treasury he watched over the coffins of Tutankhamun and the treasures filling the room around him.

This golden cow's head carved from a block of wood was found partly wrapped in linen near the doorway of the Treasury.

The graceful figure of the goddess Selket is one of four goddesses placed on each side of the golden shrine. Her sign is the scorpion seen on top of her head. She was believed to be able to cure scorpion bites.

This is the chest found inside the shrine. It was made from a solid block of alabaster. Four compartments were carved out of the inside.

This golden shrine is over six feet tall and sits upon a massive sled. Sleds were sometimes used to transport large objects over the desert sand.

Each of the four compartments had an alabaster stopper in the shape of the head and shoulders of Tutankhamun.

Inside the chest the four compartments can be seen. Each one was filled with a linen-wrapped small coffin.

This small coffin is one of four containing the internal organs of Tutankhamun. The four coffins were beautifully inlaid with glass paste and stones.

This mirror case is in the shape of an ankh, the Egyptian symbol of life. The word for mirror was also ankh. The actual mirror was missing, probably taken by thieves.

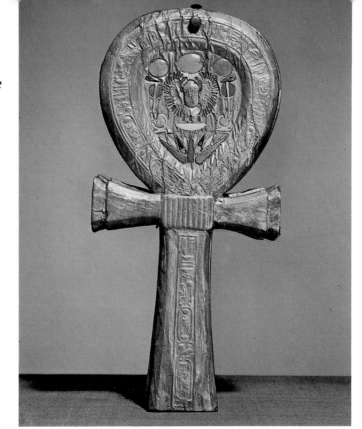

All the equipment for writing hieroglyphs was found in this small box made of reeds. It even contained cakes of red and black ink when Carter found it. The wooden case to hold writing reeds is shaped like a column and inlaid with stones and glass.

The solid gold statue shown at left hung from a chain. It is not certain if it represents Tutankhamun or one of the kings before him, Amenhotpe III. It was found wrapped in linen around a small coffin which held a lock of hair from a former queen, Tiye.

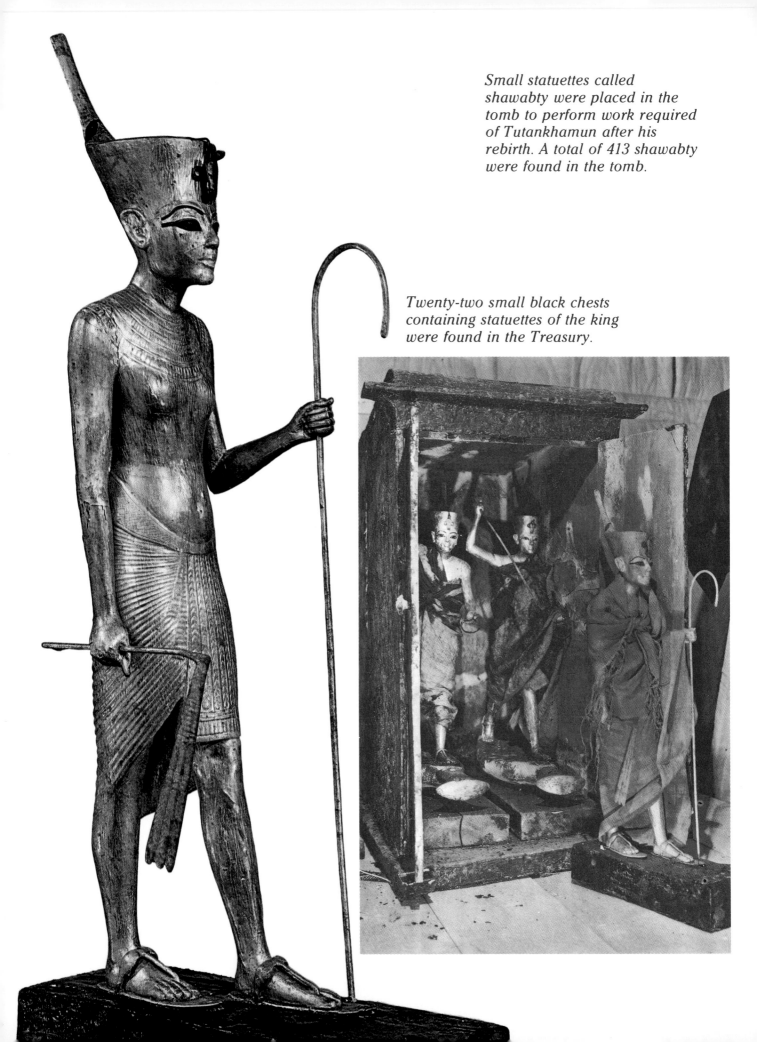

Small statuettes called shawabty were placed in the tomb to perform work required of Tutankhamun after his rebirth. A total of 413 shawabty were found in the tomb.

Twenty-two small black chests containing statuettes of the king were found in the Treasury.

Chests filled with jewels were found in the Treasury. This one shows the superb workmanship of the ancient Egyptian craftsmen. The sacred eye represents rebirth.

Boys in Egypt wore earrings. This pair was probably worn by Tutankhamun when he was a child.

This may be a model of the
boat that took the dead
Tutankhamun from his palace
to a dock near the Valley of
the Kings.

A small wooden model of the
king lying on his funerary bed
was a gift from Maya, one of
Tutankhamun's officials. On
each side is carved a bird with
a wing lying protectively over
the body of the king.

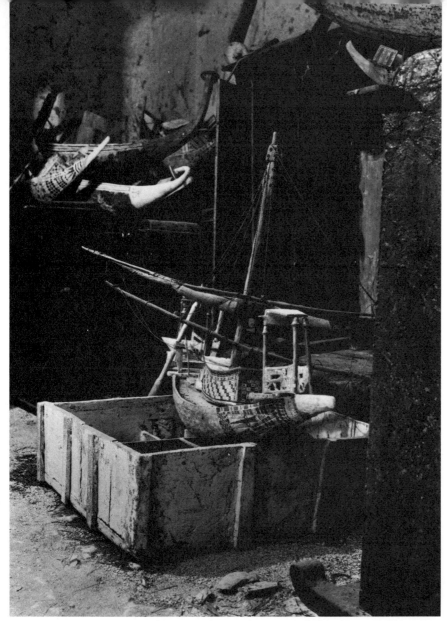

This photograph shows the boat on the left as it was found by Carter in the Treasury. Egyptians were among the best mariners of their times. They sailed not only up and down the Nile, but out to the Mediterranean Sea to trade with other lands.

Carter made his first inspection of the Annex through this hole made by thieves thousands of years earlier.

Five years after Carter first entered the tomb of Tutankhamun, he began the task of clearing the final room, the Annex. Thieves had broken into this small storeroom, and Carter made his first inspection of the room through the hole they had left. Here he found every kind of funeral object, all left helter-skelter around the room. There was hardly an object that did not show traces of the burglars. On one large box Carter could still see the very footprint of one of the last thieves.

More than three hundred objects had to be cleared before Carter's task was completed.

On the following pages are some of the beautiful treasures found in the Annex.

The use of this elaborate alabaster boat is unknown. It may have been a container for scent or perhaps a palace ornament. The ibex heads at the prow and stern of the boat have real horns.

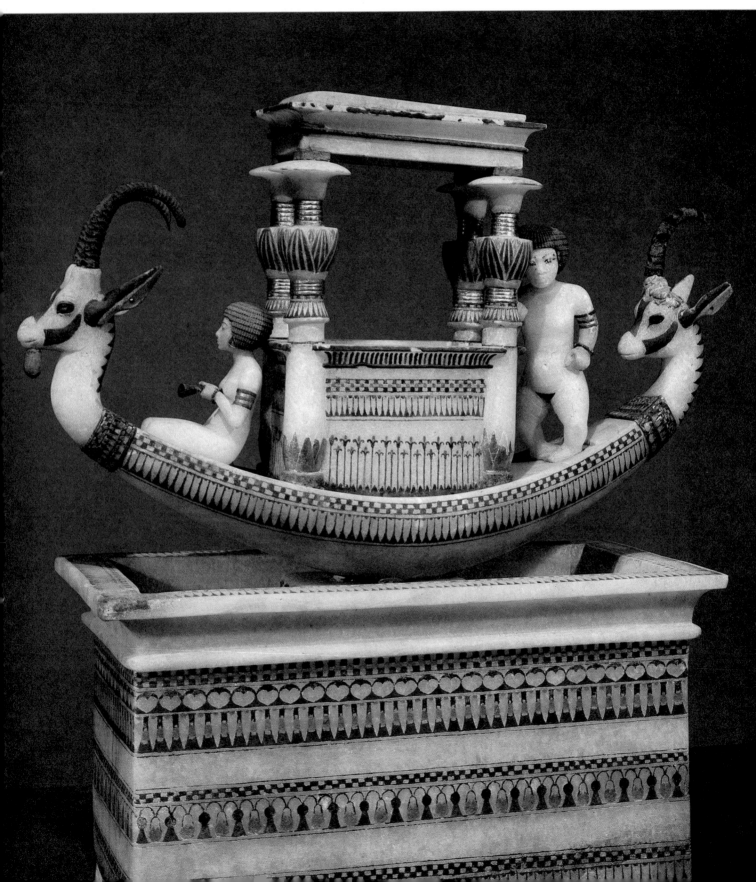

This throne is believed to have been used by Tutankhamun during religious ceremonies. Its curved seat is designed to hold a pillow. The legs represent the neck and head of wild ducks.

Thirty-four vases similar to this one were found in the Annex. Thieves had emptied most of them of their precious oils and perfumes.

Two game boards were found in the Annex. This one was called senet. The players tried to move their counters to special squares. The Egyptians did not have dice, but they played senet and other games by throwing sticks on which numbers were painted.

88

THE GOLDEN KING

Who was Tutankhamun, this king buried with so many riches?

Actually, he probably was not a very important king. It is lucky for us that he wasn't considered important. Otherwise, Howard Carter would have never found his tomb under the ground with so many of its treasures undisturbed.

How did it happen that Tutankhamun's tomb was buried, its entrance hidden for centuries?

It might have been the result of a dirt slide off the slopes of the hills that surround the Valley. More likely, the priests or officials, who controlled the Valley and supervised the laborers who were working there, had it covered after the two robberies. Or possibly it was covered when the tomb of Ramesses VI was built higher up on the hillside.

The tomb of Ramesses VI was much larger than Tutankhamun's. As a matter of fact, most of the rulers of ancient Egypt during its long history had larger and richer tombs than Tutankhamun's.

Yet the splendor of the other kings did not last long after their deaths. Their graves were robbed of almost everything that had been placed in them. Tutankhamun's was not.

Tutankhamun was king for only nine or ten years.

He was crowned king in 1334 B.C. when he was nine years old, and he probably was eighteen when he died. No doubt his advisors ruled for him during a large part of his reign.

While we do not know much about Tutankhamun, we do know a few interesting things. These were learned from hieroglyphic inscriptions and from clues found in the tomb.

He was five feet six inches in height. This is not especially tall for a man today, but then it was above average. Most Egyptians would have had to look up at him.

When he was made king, he was still a rather chubby little boy. As he reached his teens, however, he developed into a slender young man who was fond of athletics. In particular, he loved to hunt and to drive chariots.

He was married at a very early age. Tutankhamun did not have much choice in the matter. His bride was chosen for him. She had to be from the royal family. A king could not marry just anyone he pleased. After his death he was supposed to change into a god, and even during his life he was thought of as a god-man. Only a woman of royalty could marry a god.

Yet his wife, Ankhesenpaaton (she was later to change her name to Ankhesenamun), and he grew to love each other. In many of the scenes in the tomb, such as the hunting pictures on the little golden shrine, they are shown clearly enjoying each other's company. She was a slender and beautiful young woman.

This solid gold statue of the king as a boy was found wrapped in linen in the Burial Chamber. A silver statue almost like it was found along with it on the floor between the first and second shrines.

The king and queen are shown together in many of the lovely scenes decorating the small golden shrine found in the Antechamber.

A small bunch of flowers had been found on top of the first coffin. Dried and wilted after thousands of years, they still had faint colors. Carter believed that they were placed there by the young king's mourning wife.

Tutankhamun left no sons to take the throne. Yet it is curious that the mummies of two babies were also found in the tomb. Some archeologists believe that these were not the king's children, but were put there as part of the funeral ceremony.

No one knows what caused Tutankhamun's death. Some modern writers think he might have been poisoned. There is no proof of this, though, nor any proof that Tutankhamun was so disliked that anyone wished to do away with him. And it is true that many of his relatives, including his older brother, died at an early age.

Although Tutankhamun's reign as king was short, he did make one very important decision that brought peace to the troubled land of Egypt.

The king just before Tutankhamun was one of the most interesting rulers in history. His name when he was crowned was Amenhotpe IV. That name in English means "Amun is satisfied."

Amun was the chief god among the many gods the Egyptians worshipped. But Amenhotpe brought a new idea of Egyptian religion — the worship of only one god who was the divine ruler over all things. This was a very advanced idea, but it was to bring a great deal of turmoil to Egypt.

The new god was named Aton. To honor him, Amenhotpe changed his name to Akhenaton, which means "It goes well with Aton."

Now that might have been all right if that was all Akenaton had done. But he did far more. The capital of Thebes was not only the place where the king lived and ruled, but also a holy city of Egypt. It was the headquarters of the priests of Amun. Akhenaton moved his government away from Thebes and created a new capital city, which he called Akhetaton.

Akhenaton went even further. He ordered that the names of Amun and the other gods be scratched out on all walls throughout the land. Also, the various sects of rich and powerful priests who worshipped these gods were no longer allowed to practice their religion. Their temples were closed.

These fast changes were very puzzling to most Egyptians. Should they follow the religion of the king, or should they listen to the priests of Amun and refuse? They owed loyalty to their king Akhenaton, but they were far from sure that his one god, Aton, would bring them safely to the beautiful land they had been promised after death.

It is difficult to say what might have happened if Akenaton had lived longer. His idea might have succeeded. On the other hand, there might have been a bloody civil war in Egypt.

The face of Akhenaton has been carved on a piece of limestone. It was found by Petrie in 1891 at Tell el Armana which had been Akhenaton's capital city.

But Akhenaton died, and Tutankhamun took his place. The young king had been brought up at the court in Akhetaton. His name then was Tutankh*aton* and his wife's name was Akhesenpa*aton.*

Three years after he became king, he changed his name to Tutankh*amun.* He left the lovely new city and went to Thebes. The temple of Amun was opened once more.

It is probable that this decision was not the young ruler's alone, but was also that of his chief adviser, Ay, the grandfather of his wife.

Yet it is true that Tutankhamun brought calm to a land that was on the edge of civil war. He restored its traditional religion and returned the priests to their high positions. These accomplishments must have made him very popular with the people during his short reign.

The richness of his burial mask and coffins and the treasures that surrounded him in his tomb reflect the high esteem in which he was held. The personal touches — the dried flowers on his mummy, the lock of hair in a box, his favorite games, his childhood chair, and other sentimental mementos — indicate that King Tutankhamun was loved as well as honored.

Tutankhamun's childhood chair was found on the floor of the Antechamber.